LIFE ON EARTH!
Biodiversity Explained

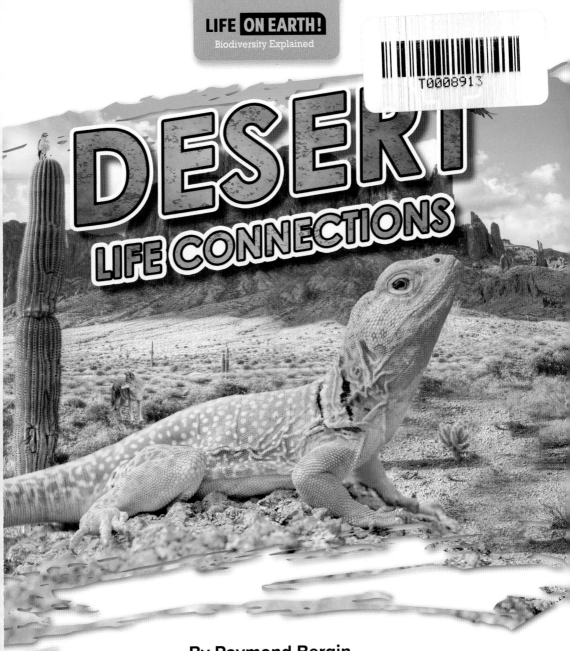

DESERT
LIFE CONNECTIONS

By Raymond Bergin

BEARPORT
PUBLISHING

Minneapolis, Minnesota

Credits

Cover and Title page © Joe Belanger/Alamy, © GracedByTheLight/Getty Images, © Zeiss4Me/iStock , © Edgar Figueiredo/iStock, © Rafael Cerqueira/iStock, © Dr John A Horsfall/iStock; 4–5, © Nimit Virdi/Getty Images; 6, © Shakeel Sha/iStock; 6–7, © benedek/Getty Images; 8, © Wojciech Dziadosz/Shutterstock; 8–9, © Phonix_a Pk.sarote/Shutterstock; 10, © Nicholas Taffs/Shutterstock; 10–11, © JohanSwanepoel/Adobe Stock; 12–13, © JeffGoulden/iStock; 14–15, © byllwill/iStock; 16–17, © Linda Johnsonbaugh Arizona /Alamy; JTE7HX 17, © krblokhin/iStock; 18, © Bill Gorum / Alamy; 18–19, © Different_Brian/Getty Images; 20–21, © PPAMPicture/iStock; 22–23, © guenterguni/Getty Images; 24–25, © Robert Landau/Alamy; 25, © helovi/iStock; 26–27, © George Ostertag/Alamy; 28, © ozgurdonmaz/iStock; 29 step 1, © JannHuizenga/iStock; 29 step 2, © stellalevi/iStock; 29 step 3, © vasiliki/iStock; 29 step 4, © simonkr/iStock; 29 step 5, © VlarVix/iStock.

Bearport Publishing Company Product Development Team
President: Jen Jenson; Director of Product Development: Spencer Brinker; Senior Editor: Allison Juda; Editor: Charly Haley; Associate Editor: Naomi Reich; Senior Designer: Colin O'Dea; Associate Designer: Elena Klinkner; Associate Designer: Kayla Eggert; Product Development Assistant: Anita Stasson

Library of Congress Cataloging-in-Publication Data

Names: Bergin, Raymond, 1968- author.
Title: Desert life connections / by Raymond Bergin.
Description: Minneapolis, Minnesota : Bearport Publishing Company, [2023] | Series: Life on Earth! Biodiversity explained | Includes bibliographical references and index.
Identifiers: LCCN 2022034471 (print) | LCCN 2022034472 (ebook) | ISBN 9798885094092 (library binding) | ISBN 9798885095310 (paperback) | ISBN 9798885096461 (ebook)
Subjects: LCSH: Desert biology--Juvenile literature. | Desert ecology--Juvenile literature.
Classification: LCC QH88 .B47 2023 (print) | LCC QH88 (ebook) | DDC 577.54--dc23/eng/20220808
LC record available at https://lccn.loc.gov/2022034471
LC ebook record available at https://lccn.loc.gov/2022034472

For more information, write to Bearport Publishing, 5357 Penn Avenue South, Minneapolis, MN 55419

Contents

Signs of Life

A desert may seem like nothing but sand and dust as far as the eye can see. But look more closely—it is full of life. A mouse crouches in the shade of a shrub while a hungry snake hides in the sand nearby, waiting patiently for a rodent snack. Overhead, a bird swoops down to a watering hole. There, **predators** and **prey** alike find relief under the scorching sun.

But in the distance, machinery roars and there is a faint smell of wildfire smoke. The desert is in danger. What's happening to life on Earth?

Within Arizona's Sonoran Desert alone, there is an incredible variety of life. Across this desert, you can find 350 **species** of birds, 60 types of mammals, 100 kinds of reptiles, and 2,000 different plant varieties.

A Planet Full of Life

Earth is covered in many biomes—areas of land and sea where the **climate** and natural features are a perfect fit for certain kinds of plants and animals. Tundras, grasslands, forests, wetlands, oceans, and deserts are all biomes.

Every biome is home to a connected community of life. This wide variety of connected life is called **biodiversity**. Each desert biome can include everything from tiny, leafless **succulents** to towering yucca trees and lumbering elephants.

Tortoises rely on desert plants for food, water, and shade. In turn, they share their burrows with gila monsters, roadrunners, and owls.

What Is a Desert?

Biodiversity looks different in deserts around the globe, but all deserts share one thing in common. They don't get much water. Deserts are dry! They usually have less than 10 inches (25 cm) of rain or snow a year. The rain that *does* fall seeps through the soil quickly, leaving the surface of the ground dry shortly after a shower. Under a hot desert sun, the amount of water that **evaporates** from soil and plant surfaces is often greater than the yearly rainfall.

Parts of Antarctica are considered deserts. No new snow or rain has fallen in some cold, dry spots for 14 million years!

Not Deserted

With such extreme heat and little water, surviving in a desert is really hard. Yet, thousands of plants and animals have found ways to make it work. Some of them depend upon watering holes.

These desert lifelines form when elephants dig into termite mounds for a meal. The big beasts leave behind large hollows where the mounds once were. These holes eventually fill with rainwater, and dozens of kinds of desert animals—from bats and birds to lions and giraffes—gather to enjoy a refreshing drink.

Watering holes can be few and far between in deserts. As such, some animals have learned to live without water. Kangaroo rats never drink a single drop. They get all their water from their food.

It All Fits Together

From termites to elephants, each living thing in the desert is important for the survival of the rest. Desert plants give cooling shade, store valuable water, and provide rare **nutrients** for little desert creatures. Small animals are a source of food for larger ones. Even after death, organisms break down and help more desert plants grow. Sandy survival depends on the help offered by other desert dwellers.

The Gila woodpecker and the saguaro cactus work together. The cactus provides a home for the bird. In return, the woodpecker eats the diseased parts of the cactus and snacks on insects that are harmful to the plant.

A Gila woodpecker perched on a saguaro cactus

Deserts in Danger

When these life connections are disrupted, desert biomes become weaker. If even one little part of a desert changes, a chain reaction can start that harms hundreds of plants and animals.

Unfortunately, conditions in the desert are changing. Rising temperatures worldwide are making deserts even hotter and drier. Some of the land is being taken over by cities or turned into farms. Hunters are killing desert animals illegally. The desert's delicate web of life is getting torn.

There are almost 1,500 species of cacti, but one-third of them are threatened with **extinction** due to increasing heat, **development**, and human harvesting. Cacti are more **endangered** than Earth's mammals!

Even Hotter and Drier

It's hard to imagine that desert heat could get any more extreme. However, every time we burn fuel to power cars, homes, and factories, we release **carbon dioxide** into the air. Once there, it traps Earth's heat, making temperatures rise. Desert life can't always handle this new heat.

When it's too hot, desert plants shrivel up without flowering. That spells trouble for the animals that rely on these plants for shade and food. Many die, and those that do survive must spend their time staying cool rather than **mating**. Soon, the desert is missing an entire generation of creatures.

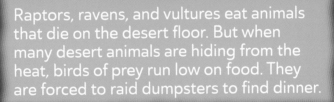

Raptors, ravens, and vultures eat animals that die on the desert floor. But when many desert animals are hiding from the heat, birds of prey run low on food. They are forced to raid dumpsters to find dinner.

I Was Going to Eat That!

Despite the heat, humans have also taken over the desert for our own uses. To meet our ever-growing food needs, farmers and ranchers are moving into deserts—and disrupting the life already there.

Oak trees in the Chihuhuan Desert offer food, shade, and protection to dunes sagebrush lizards. But the trees make cattle sick. Ranchers get rid of the trees with a poison that is harmful to both the trees and the lizards.

In the Chihuhuan Desert along the United States-Mexico border, **livestock** are destroying the **native** plants and grasses that wild desert mammals depend upon for survival. As a result, these animals are disappearing. Chihuhuan brown bears and some of the smaller animals that feed on the plants have died out completely. Big cats that feed on **herbivores** have also disappeared.

Ranched cattle and sheep often trample many of the plants they don't eat.

When Humans Move In

Roads, homes, and businesses are also spreading into desert areas. To make room for the human structures, we're tearing out **vegetation** that is vital to the survival of desert wildlife.

Without cacti, nesting birds, such as woodpeckers, owls, and even hawks, lose their homes. Rats, rabbits, deer, and sheep can't find enough food or water. If cactus flowers are gone, then the bats, bees, insects, and birds that rely on their nectar also leave. These animals will not be around to carry pollen to help create new plants.

When people move to the desert, they build roads and drive vehicles that destroy soil and plants. This causes coyotes to move away from their dens in the damaged land and owls and falcons to abandon their nests.

Death in the Desert

One of the leading causes of species loss in deserts is **poaching**—illegally hunting animals. Some of the most frequently poached desert animals are also some of the most important animals for keeping desert life in balance.

Lions kill herbivores, such as buffalo and zebras, stopping them from eating all the desert plants. They also kill the weakest animals that are most likely to carry and spread diseases. If the lions are killed, the number of plant-eating animals can grow out of control.

Elephants are poached for their tusks. But these large animals trample the desert floor in a way that provides food and shelter for small desert creatures. Without them, small animals suffer.

We Need Deserts

Life on Earth is all connected. If deserts and their wildlife become unhealthy, so will we. In fact, one billion people—one out of seven people around the world—live in deserts! Desert plants protect these people and their homes from severe weather. Their roots keep water-absorbing soil in place. Without them, the soil dries out and blows away, causing dust storms or flooding that harm nearby neighborhoods and settlements.

Desert animals have carried humans and their loads for thousands of years. Desert plants have fed us and been used as medicines for even longer.

Desert Life Returns

All over the world, people are beginning to recognize how important the wide variety of desert life is to the health of the entire planet. Native desert vegetation is being replanted in areas where it had previously been torn out. Poachers are being punished, and scientists are helping threatened animals have more babies. More desert land is being protected.

Surviving in the desert is really hard, but we are finding ways to make it just a little easier. We owe our lives to the life connections found in the deserts.

The Desert National Wildlife Refuge in Nevada is more than twice the size of Rhode Island. It provides a protected home for 500 plant, 320 bird, 52 mammal, and 32 reptile species.

Save the Desert

What can we do to save the deserts? If we reduce the amount of heat-trapping carbon dioxide we make and protect desert plants and animals, we can take a huge step in the right direction.

Visit protected natural areas and wildlife refuges to support their creation and expansion.

When hiking or driving in deserts, stay on marked trails, paths, and roadways.

Conserve water. Take short showers and avoid using sprinklers to water your lawn. Instead, plant native plants that require little human care.

If it is possible and safe, walk, ride a bike, or take public transportation to get where you're going instead of releasing heat-trapping carbon dioxide into the air with your car.

Electricity is often made by burning fuel. Save electricity by turning off lights and unplugging electronics when you're not using them.

Glossary

biodiversity the existence of many different kinds of plants and animals in an environment

carbon dioxide a gas given off when fossil fuels are burned

climate the typical weather in a place

development the use of land for human activity, commonly including building new construction

endangered close to being killed or dying off completely

evaporates turns from a liquid to a gas

extinction when a type of animal or plant dies out

herbivores animals that eat only plants

livestock animals raised on farms or ranches, such as cows, sheep, and goats

mating coming together in order to have young

native originally belonging to a certain place

nutrients vitamins, minerals, and other substances needed by living things for health and growth

poaching hunting illegally

predators animals that hunt and eat other animals

prey animals that are hunted by other animals for food

species groups that animals and plants are divided into according to similar characteristics

succulents plants that save and store water

vegetation plant life

Read More

Bergin, Raymond. *Animals in Danger (What on Earth? Climate Change Explained).* Minneapolis: Bearport Publishing, 2022.

Griffin, Mary. *Prickly Desert Cacti (Fantastic Plants).* New York: PowerKids Press, 2023.

Keppeler, Jill. *20 Fun Facts About Desert Habitats (Fun Fact File: Habitats).* New York: Gareth Stevens Publishing, 2022.

Nargi, Lela. *Desert Biomes (Exploring Biomes).* Minneapolis: Jump!, 2023.

Learn More Online

1. Go to **www.factsurfer.com** or scan the QR code below.

2. Enter "**Desert Connections**" into the search box.

3. Click on the cover of this book to see a list of websites.

Index

About the Author

In the early 1970s, Raymond's family station wagon broke down in Death Valley, California—one of the hottest places on Earth. While waiting for a tow truck, Raymond didn't spot much life, but, now that he has learned more about deserts, he wishes he could go back and take a much closer look.